# All I Cannot See

*The Words and Thoughts of Arnim Nicolson*

ISBN: 978-1-7923-1694-4

Cover art by Diana Forster.
Book and cover design by Leisha Babayan.

www.ArnimNicolson.com

# Contents

## Others

## God & Jesus Christ

# Forward

*All I Cannot See*, the words and thoughts of Arnim Nicolson has been one of my most loved and challenging poetry books. As a child and in high school I read much literature and poetry including Elizabeth Browning, Robert Frost, etc. but never felt as challenged as I had until I read the God-given poetic insights of my newly found friend, Arnim Nicolson.

I first met Arnim and his wife Susan, in February 2019 through a mutual friend. I had invited this friend to stay with me for a few weeks after a surgical procedure to recuperate in my home so that she would be more comfortable. Arnim had heard that this friend was staying with me and our friend invited Arnim and his wife over for a visit.

I will always be grateful for this invitation that was given to the Nicolson's because it began my journey into reading the poetic words that I never could have imagined would come from such a seasoned professional man as Arnim. Such readings not only speak to my heart but also expand my desire to read more and more of these poetic works that Arnim is creating daily!

I loved the seriousness of our conversations as Arnim sat in my home for hours and hours expressing how he felt as he wrote his poetry. Our discussions brought out welcomed questions and stories followed that flowed with his life. He gave vivid explanations of how he was able to put pen to paper and give countless stories about God, his creator, as he describes Him in his poetic writings.

I marveled as the pages turned and Arnim pointed out how the blessings that came daily from his God-given gifts. What an inspiration this was and still is to me as an enthusiast of his work.

Arnim is a very strong advocate of the Gospel. He put his words to rhythmic motions, never losing his vision and compassion as he writes; evident in the beautifully placed poetry on each page of this book.

I have certainly come to enjoy and love God's words through this wonderful man of God in the greater South Valley of the Bay. Thank you Arnim for asking me to be a support system; to talk to and share, to show my appreciation for this complicated gift that the Lord has definitely given you. Thank you for sharing with all of us who love poetry or who want to understand poetry more.

Enjoy readers, and ask lots of questions as you read. Mark your pages and enjoy each page of enthusiastic words, may they empower you to write your own words of encouragement to share with the world as Arnim has done.

- Dr. Dee C. Robinson

# Preface

This is my creation as given to me by those of another world or as I would say, out of the world of thoughts. It has been a gift from God that I have been able to gather out of the world of thoughts these poems and short stories.

There is a God and His Son Jesus Christ and they have left me with the ability to put these words on paper. The journey has been just amazing to me as it has been borne to others who know me.

These words and thoughts are my testimony of their existence. Without them, there would not be words or thoughts to write.

May you ponder upon them as I did. It would be my hope and prayer that you would feel the peace that came to me as I wrote them.

- Arnim Nicolson

# Men & Women

# The Men Who Came to Pray

Who are these men that come to pray
Close the door and let us pray
They have waited long for me to pray
All as one then I began to pray
I thanked the Father for each and every one
They only listened as I began to pray
Names long forgotten and ones I knew
I felt their pain what was I to do
Pen in hand I just began to list their names
Then I knew each and every one
Unlock this door and set us free
Their thoughts were loud and clear
Was I bound by this priesthood oath so long ago
Was I the only one to set them free
One by one their names reappeared upon my mind
Names dates places wives' children
Each of them were a part of me
I knew I held the key for their prison door
In a temple they could be free
What was I to do except set them free
Now their work is done
No longer do they come to pray

# A Good Woman

Gold is good but cold and land is good but hard to work
Water is good to drink food comes and goes
Men go to war to fight night turns to light
A good woman is hard to find

Some have good minds some are tall some are short
Then there is this, Good women or mine
She loves my mind she cares for me
She tries her best her love is fine

Songs to sing what a treat it brings to me
Children at her feet this makes her smile
Her tender spirit from above was sent to me
Not too short not too tall just right for me

Her mind refined was a guide to mine
Her patience was tried while I tried to find my peace of mind
Each year that passed she smiled at me
I know true love when she holds my hand

It is her spirit that speaks to me not a word she says
The message is loud and clear
God has sent me here to comfort you
With us two, will bring you through

Life can be a trial if left to walk alone
Is hard to find some comfort with gold alone
Tis cold at night when left alone
Why cook when you'll all alone

What warmth is their when home alone
So if God would smile on you
To send to you a good woman
I would hope he could find one as good as mine

There are few that knows the minds of men
Like this one of mine
It is her love of God that refines her mind
Her gentle smile her tender heart

If she wrinkles up her nose she has to be a clone of mine
There is only one like mine, which brings great joy
It is our peace of mind that brings this joy
For you see we are married for all eternity.

# All Alone

How can a person be all alone
Surrounded by this mass of humanity
Why was Adam left all alone
Within God's garden so long ago

Could it be the same for Adam and us
So many places to roam
Yet one can be left all alone

What was God's response to those
Who think they are all alone
"It is not good for man to be alone"

Then God asked Adam what he would give
That he might not be alone
A rib that's close to my heart

So the surgery began very close to his heart
When God had finished-- Adam exclaimed
I now have a help mate that's very close to my heart

So it is with us when we feel all alone
What would we give not to be all alone
If not a piece of our heart

So let the search begin to help a broken heart
Piece it back together with a love divine
What God did for Adam he can do for us

When we place our heart in God's tender care
You too soon will exclaim  I now have a help mate
If not you might be left all alone

In a world that keeps on asking
What was it that God said
"It is not good for man to be alone"

# A Soldier

Father son daughter country men
Alive and well or dead on a battlefield
Friend or foe are they not all alike
Men of courage men of skill
Young or old born of a mother
One of God's children born to live and die
Men alive to tell their tale
A name on a tombstone in some foreign place
Telling their tale in another place
Some broken and lame
Safe now from the battlefield
Others safe on the other side
Free from this life's battlefield
Are they now friend and foe
Within God's presence
Fresh from the battlefields
Give these soldiers time to rest
They have just found themselves
In a foreign place
No longer weapons in hand
Standing in the presence of God
With how many soldiers from the past
Friend and foe no longer
Basking in God's eternal light
Now they understand who was right
Basking in God's eternal light

# A Soldier's Nurse

A life to save a life to give there's always hope
Infirmity is not my lot how soon will it end
Voices faint lights so dim is it the end
A tender touch a soft voice

Is it real or just a dream
A voice of comfort love unfeigned
Are you an angel no just your nurse
Will I live or will I die

Hold my hand and close your eyes
Memories of a mother's touch
This soldier is still alive
Nurse is there any hope

Your life you gave to save a brother
You're almost home squeeze my hand
Nurse God has him now
God please bless that nurse of mine

# Man And His IQ

What is man if not an intelligent soul
Who can define his intelligent mind

Did not God organize this mortal man
Then how can man determine his intelligence

Man's philosophies and his IQ it's just a test
But the seeking soul of humble repentant man

Has God's attention for wisdom and eternal light
When man knows of God's existence

Then the intelligence of man really begins to grow
Who can turn water into quality wine with just a word

Who can raise the dead with just a command
Who can heal the broken body with just a touch

Who can ascend from galaxy to earth
In a column of light to communicate with man

If not the creator of us all
When man acquires these gifts

O the intelligence of that man
So it is with the quest of man to know this God

If only he would become a humble repentant soul
Then his eyes of understanding would start to grow

Yet man seems to resist this quest
He would rather rely on his IQ and settle for so much less

So it is with life and man's intelligence
God has said he is more intelligent than us all

Why then should man settle for less
If God offers man eternal life

# Man's Imagination

Is there anything unimaginable
For the soul of man
Where does man's imagination dwell
Is it real or just a dream

When and where does it go
Is it the same for each and every soul
Could there be no limit to one's imagination
Let your imagination grow and grow

It is an integral part of the human soul
Like the God that no one sees
Was His gift that man might see
Throughout His galaxies

Is it locked within some prison cell
Or is it alive and functioning well
You're the master of your soul
Let your imagination dwell upon things unseen

God is alive and well
Your imagination is your passport
To view beyond the veil of things unseen
God's imagination was free

What good is a gift locked within a prison cell
Like the human soul that no one sees
It will be man's imagination that lets him view
Of God's beloved Son hanging on a tree

Now dwelling as a resurrected soul
In some far-off galaxy
Man's imagination is alive and well
Dwelling within his eternal soul

Without your imagination
How bleak the human soul would be

# Since She Has Left

Since she has left the sunset is still the same
Yet different somehow
The table & chairs still the same
Yet different since she has left
Her pillow sits so still the same as yesterday
When I lay my head next to it it's not the same
When I call her name it sounds the same
Yet what I hear is not the same
Somehow when she left all things have changed
I used to think she made a mess
Now that she is gone it's too clean
When I cook the food it's still the same
Yet when I set the plate there's only one
The foods just not the same
I walk our path and see all things as yesterday
Yet it's different now
When I walk within our home everything is in its place
Yet something's different now
I kneel to pray, reach to touch her hand
It's gone, the tears run down my face
I miss her smile her voice it's too quiet
What will I do now that she is gone
Who will fill her space
Who will comfort me when sad and blue
What will I do when I look for her
Then realize she has left
Listen my child to your Heavenly Father wise and true

My love and comfort has no end
It's a vision of things to be
When upon a bended knee and you call to Me
I'll send the comforter
He has the power to wipe away those tears
Give vision of things yet to be
Reveal to view the one who left
Memory of things you shared
Your children you brought to earth
The memory of her voice
I'll send her near when your heart needs comfort
She'll watch your tears as they disappear
Then time will come when the one who left
Will be her voice you shall hear
All clothed in white with power from on high
She's here with Me
Beyond the veil in My eternity
You're still within our view
It's your faith that knows I do exist
When you feel that peace and comfort
That's when you will know
She is near to you
Until it's time for you to come and be with us
Have faith my son she waits patiently
Just as My Son Jesus Christ
Who waits for all when it's time to leave

# Tender Hands

Where have all the tender hands gone
Once young and tender were they
Each child with their tender hands
O how tender hands and tender hearts
Seemed to go together

When did they become hardened and out of reach
Each child of God so young and sweet
Each mother and her child holding hands
When did they separate this mother and her child
No longer holding hands

What became of that tender heart
How does a hardened heart change a tender hand
O how they used to kneel and pray
Then time seemed to separate these hands

Now only the mother seems to pray
That her child would hold her hand
What causes one to cease to pray
If not a hardened heart

Far from a mother's hand to touch
Each day the distance between the two
Grows harder and harder and out of reach
If only the child would stop and pray
Then the Master could soften up their heart

Then the distance to their mother's hand
Wouldn't seem so far
Like the Savior -- holding the mother's hand
Each waiting for those tender hands
Once again to reappear

Who will replace the mother's hand
When the child begins to pray
If not the Savior of all mankind
Who but He -- that has the tender heart
Will hold the child when he begins to pray

# Trapped

In a world of restraint a mortal soul
A physical immovable body
Is there no escape for me what am I to do
No movable parts and bounded within

No place to go no place to hide
Stuck within this chair of mine
Is there no one to care where should I go
Why am I even alive

O how I wish I could fly off to some foreign place
Walk upon a beach and feel some sand
Yet here I sit trapped within my chair
If only I could feel my toes what good are my arms

No more do they move, O- how I hate being trapped
Then came to my mind
You have unlimited power
Close your eyes activate your mind

There is no power to match the human mind
Capable imagining almost anything
What is time but a place to reside
Yet your mind has never been trapped

It resides within for such a short time
Soon freed and already to go
No longer trapped within a world of Woe
No longer trapped within a mortal soul

Now free to explore God's mysteries
Throughout God's galaxies and beyond
In a resurrected perfected body
Thus the mind has achieved its dream

Once again whole and complete
Living on some secluded beach
Feeling the sand on each and every toe
For in God's world each soul is complete

# The Scotsman

Far away from his home across the sea
To the land of liberty
Came this Scotsman
In a land where he could roam

Over the sea on ship he came
Hammer in hand was this blacksmith man
Found his bride for they were meant to be
Now to the land that would be their new home

Down to the frontier they came
Vision in his mind of things to be
Hotel stable blacksmith shop
Family well on their way

Welcome to Cole Camp for they were here to stay
All went well until one day
There came to town these rabid dogs
The Scotsman stood his ground

But the dog had won the round
Now what to do was his first clue
Off to find the mad stone man
Was not to be the doctor said

Back to his home he came knowing what to do
Off to the prison cell confined and safe
Was the wisdom of this Scotsman
His children all around prayer was heard

Then he sent them far away
For not to hear his cries of anguish
For you see his blood runs
Within my veins

Just like our Savior we all will suffer
Just a little bit of pain
But for this Scotsman I exist
Thanks be his name

# Mysteries of Men

# Time and Beauty

Time versus beauty which came first
Somewhere in time when it all started
Time and beauty went hand in hand
Then the journey it began
In the making of a soul
Who is the designer of our soul
If not the Creator of us all
Who can criticize the Creator of a soul
When he holds time and beauty
Within His Holy hand
God had brought them together
This time and beauty His making of a soul
Now you see His handy work
Young and old yet time and beauty
They will always go hand in hand
Let the Master of our soul
Continue to form this human soul
Only time will tell the beauty of this soul
Let the Creator have full control
It will surprise you when it's finished
This beauty and its time
When resurrected into an immortal soul
Then placed upon a world of like-kind
Who will be the Judge of your beauty
If not the Creator of your soul

# Accountability

The gift of moral agency is just the beginning
Humankind had its beginning long before
God bestowed upon man His agency
Accountability will always follow responsibly

With moral agency comes eternal laws
Who is man to ignore these laws
With God's gift comes accountability
Alive or dead man will stand accountable

There is a time to plant a time to sow a time to reap
Long before man became a human soul he agreed
To accept this agency and its accountability
God is the master gardener of our soul

Planted He us here with moral agency
We become the sowers of our agency
Accountability will be the reaper of our soul
Justice waits for our accountability day

Eternal laws will always demand justice
Where then is mercy for a sinful soul
In the days of accountability
Eternal laws require a humble repentant soul

In the days before his accountability
Moral agency has its responsibility for every human soul
Without moral agency what is man
But a seed unplanted with no responsibility

Use God's gift of moral agency wisely
It will determine the
Destiny of your soul
For eternity is a very long time

# All I Cannot See

What can I see when it lies beyond my view
The world doth turn the sun doth shine
Worlds come and go yet these stars still shine
How can I see what I do not see

Is a thought real or just a dream
Can you hold God's time
You tell me of things I cannot see
How can they be real if I think they do not exist

I exist because of men long gone
Men come and go yet here I stand
Who came that I could exist I saw them not
Yet here am I for all to view yet soon I leave

Then will I be real far from your view
Yet your eyes won't see this man I used to be
Yet for me I will exist some place in time
You'll read these words they'll stretch your mind

Could you exist if I saw you not
What is real if you think it's not
What exists as yet undiscovered
When you leave mortality

Will thoughts and time become a reality
Who controls our destiny
Is it you or I
Or some other Entity

One came long ago so I was told
He lived and died and rose again
Traveled throughout the eternities
Returned and said, "I will come again"

He does exist far from our view
Was God's Son He sent
To guide a humble soul
To cross this vast chasm of eternity

Close your eyes ask of Him
To view these things unseen
Tis God's power that opens up the mind
Gives man

A clear view of eternity that's unseen

# Bittersweet

Life is a marvelous journey so I have been told
With all of its water ice and snow

Gold silver diamonds and many precious things
Deserts- mountains valleys and all of its many seas

Then there is the universe with its sun moon and many stars
There seems to be no lack of variations good or bad

They all seem to exist next to one and all
Why then-- to think that things are either good or bad

Life with its many variations like you or me
Who is right or who is wrong it seems to be our song

Yet each new day brings another rising of the sun
You say my thinking is all wrong

I say the lemon is so bitter and the melon is so sweet
Who then is right or wrong

Life was meant to be a test so you tell me
What is bitter or what is sweet

If I only had the lemon and had no sweet
What would be the difference

So it is with life we all have to have some sweet
Then how can you say the bitter is not as good as the sweet

Life is not a test without this bitter and its sweet
So if you taste the bitter before the sweet

Just remember somewhere along the road
There comes a time when you will savor God's good sweet

Until that time enjoy the bitter and the sweet
Life was meant to be a test for you and me

Without the bitter and the sweet
Life wouldn't be a test

# Is Man Really Free

Locked within his prison cell
Life is just a journey

In a human mortal soul
Locked within this earthly sphere

Who then is really free
To roam the galaxies and beyond

Weighted down with this mortal ball of clay
In this earthly hemisphere

Weighted down with many human cares
Life can become a very lonely place

Locked within his prison cell
How can man escape without a door

Who then is really free to roam
If not a humble righteous soul

Man was meant to escape his prison cell
Then travel to a much higher sphere

Could death be another prison door
For the unrepentant soul

Death is just another prison cell
Locked with all of his human cares

Jesus Christ is master healer of the soul
If man truly wants his freedom

Faith in Christ has always been the door
That lets men fly to loftier spheres

Man was created that he might be free
To roam the galaxies

Free from all of these earthly cares
If he remains a humble repentant soul

# Music From Afar

Where or when did it arrive
Music that comes into the soul of man
Notes and sounds never before heard
Let the composer begin his quest

How do you explain the complexity
Of sounds you have never heard
Yet men have entertained notes from afar
Who then is the creator if not a mortal man

Sounds of every kind
To entertain the soul of man
Like the Creator of us all
Surrounded by music so pleasant to His ear

Where or when did it begin
This music from afar
Who then is the composer of it all
If not composers of another galaxy

Like the Creator of us all
Music brings joy to His soul
So it is with the mortal man
Seeking music to soothe his troubled soul

When in tune with God's beloved Son
He sends His music to soothe your soul
Then who is the composer of your music
If not your inter seeking righteous soul

Are you not the recipient of this music from afar
Then give thanks to those composers
Who know and respond to each an every
Righteous seeking soul

# The Enemy of the Soul

Listen to the Creator
Of your soul
That you might know who it is
This enemy of your soul

Always seek the light that you might see
Who it is that wants your soul
It's your prayer
That brings the light

Then cry to your Creator
That His knowledge He will send
When depression, guilt, sorrow, shame or hate
They come your way

Remember what was said
It's His light that helps the mind
To understand the
Value of the soul

You're too young to know this master of deceit
Who bargains for your soul
It's knowledge which brings the light
When you seek to know which way to go

Stop and ponder
Upon your thoughts
Then pray to see who it is
This enemy of your soul

If you're patient then seek to know
Your Creator's path which lifts the soul
Grows the mind
And brings His joy

When on your knees this prayer to give
Invite His spirit to be so near
Then your soul will understand
Who it is this enemy of the soul

It's the light of truth he fears the most
When your soul is filled with light and truth
This enemy will have to leave
Then you can start to shine for all eternity

# The Hidden You

Who is it that resides within
Where did you come from
Declare your identity
What have I to do with thee

Am I not free to roam as I please
Do you always have to annoy me
Will I never be free from thee
From my brain to my heart

You seem to be such a pain
Could you not leave me alone
What could possibly go wrong
Do you not understand

I just want to be free
To roam this world all alone
If I were to let you all alone
To roam as you please

It was meant that you and I
Were meant to be one
You on the outside me on the inside
If it wasn't for me you surely would be all alone

Now that we are together
Let us reason as one
For without each other
There surely would be no place to roam

God placed me within
That you would not be all alone
To guide and help in all that you do
With my help we can roam the world in peace

Return and live in a world of charity
So it is that you and I are one
Let the heart guide the mind in all that we do
Then we can be at peace one to another

For you and I are truly one brother
Placed on earth
So we could roam
Let us be kind to one another

Then Father will know
That you and I
Have become qualified
To be one of his sons

# The Hourglass of Time

Consider life long before it began
Housed within an hourglass of time
Each speck of sand your life's experiences
Measured in a very special way
Every thought and action
Must pass this portal of your time
Who determines when your hourglass
Begins the flow of sand
Thoughts and actions how they flow
One by one they descend
Within the hourglass of your time
Each speck of sand your experience
Accumulated
Just like a pile of sand they build
The character of your soul
Each and every action with its thoughts
Determine the destiny of your intelligence
Who holds the destiny of your hourglass
If not the Creator of your sand
If you know the Creator
Consider His different kinds of sand
For they will surely determine the destiny
And character of your soul

# The Power of Desire

I am what I am could there be more
Intelligence Desire Willingness
What shall I do with no desire
Who gives direction to willingness
Have you seen willingness at work with no desire
Who controls the power of the mind
What is the mind without intelligence
What is intelligence without desire
Only an intelligence with no place to go
What is the Soul without desire
What is life without it
Who is this entity called desire
Who gave him power over all
When God placed man on earth
It was desire He gave this control
Who then is master of the soul
If not this entity called desire
A ship with no rudder where it will go
Man and his soul with no desire
Like this ship with no rudder
Where or where with they go
Life is a journey with his precious soul
God placed desire in somewhat control
If man finds God's desire he could then
Find destiny for his eternal soul

# The Journey of an Intelligence

Into the world of thoughts
Who holds the key
The mortal body or his thoughts
Not the spirit
Only an intelligence

Light and truth throughout eternity
There is no end to intelligence
They dwell one and all
Light and truth has no end
Gather what you would

Be it light or dark surely they exist
Let my intelligence choose the light
Bring its treasure home
Into my spirit
Where does he roam

Now find my mortal soul
That all three may
Find a home
Give this mortal soul humility
Some might to write his history

Only a mortal soul with pen
Brings home his intelligence
A mortal soul
Sees more clearly
When on paper for all to see

This journey of his intelligence
God holds the key
Into the world of thoughts
There is no end to
His intelligence

Humility is our key
For the journey of an intelligence
Into the world of thoughts

# The Power of Why

Who first asked why
Who is the author of this why
What power does this why have
Who controls the power of a why

What would life be like without a why
How many whys have you asked
How many whys lie within your soul that you have not asked
What is the difference between verbalizing a why and
those you do not verbalize

When did you enter into the world of whys what
made you first ask why
Is there an answer to all whys
How does one control a why
Now that you have asked the question why -- why did you ask why

What makes an intelligence ask why and another not ask
If you never asked why where or what would you be
Could this world exist without a why
Have you ever seen this power that controls the question why

Could there be a right and wrong answer to a why
*What value do you place on your why*
How can one tell if his or her why is what the soul is searching for
What power controls your destiny in answering your why

Can you explain your why
From what source do your thoughts come to formulate your why
Is there a person who never asked the question why if so who
Now that you have asked the question where do you find the answer

If you don't understand this power then you
are still at the point of life
Where the why is still a Question
When did you stop asking why
God said let there be light

What does that have to do with the question why
If God said let there be light should not our question be why
If your spirit can comprehend that God had a reason for light to be
Then you have the capacity to understand the why

If your question is still what or who is this God
Then your why still lies within that sphere of darkness
Which only that light that He created can answer your why
May your quest be to understand the power of a why

Then may you dwell within that light that gives understanding
To all who ask why

# The World of Feelings

Explain your feelings
Mother child father
Motherhood when did it begin
Feelings you can't explain
Then they soon begin
Each and everyday
New to each of you
Explain this joy or pain
This growth that moves
What will be its name
Explain your feelings if you can
Creation when did it begin
Feelings unexplained for two
Explain the feeling of the three
Very soon the child will have a name
Each with different feelings
Yet connected just the same
Motherhood is lots of work and pain
Explain the feelings of the child
Creation is not just a game
Motherhood and life it's the same
Feelings all along the way
Thus for the child life began
Father mother child each with feelings
Yet not the same somehow
What is mortal life without these feelings
I'll let you explain somehow

# Wanted: Dead or Alive

When was man ever dead
In the beginning was man
What is man but a hand full of clay
Was not so in the beginning

Energy has no beginning so it is with man
They must go hand in hand
God's greatest work is no mystery
To bring to pass the immortality of man

There is no death only absence of energy
Seeds never die they just reemerge
In greater abundance
It is with man in a hand full of clay

Full of energy they go hand in hand
Upon this terrestrial earth
His seed never dies just reemerges
In greater abundance

When absent of clay where has his energy gone
Back to the beginning with soul in hand
Full of knowledge of God's greatest plan
Infused with greater energy for all eternity

Alive and well as an immortal soul
What is death if not just a myth?
Wanted men alive and well

# Why or What

Why do I exist?
Why does a star begin to fall?
Why does the sun stand still?
Why does God love me at all?

What made this world so special?
What sphere did I begin?
What made me, this man to see?
What kind of love does God offers me?

Why make a tree?
Why plant a sea for life to be?
Why does one cry for thee?
Why does God care for me at all?

What makes one special?
What is it that I can't see?
What gift was sent that I might be?
What peace waits for me?

Why ask me what I can't see?
Why seek to know my emptiness?
Why fill my breast with love divine?
Why seek this God of mine?

What kind of power unseen does he offer me?
What infinite love divine waits for me?
What must I do to seek?
What just ask?

Why me Lord?
Why not, you're my child?

# Winds of the Mind

Like the trees that move
Or the sand that blows
The grass that waves
White caps of a sea
Clouds that move from here to there
A cold arctic wind
A blast of desert wind
A gentle soothing breeze
All because of things unseen
Heat and cold we blame
Yet who can explain
Their source
From whence they came
From whence they go
Like thoughts upon the mind
Are we to blame
From whence they came
Will they move us --from here to there
Or like the tree that stands
Unmovable
Will your values withstand
These winds of time
Who is to blame

# Others

# The Artists

Beginning of your thoughts
Vision of your mind of things unseen
Canvas of your mind onto reality
Visions-dreams how should they be

You're the creator of your dreams
Brush and paints mixture of your mind
Brush in hand paints and canvas
May God please guide your hand

From dreams to canvas
Each stroke this canvas she's alive
Dreams of the mind
Flow upon this scene

Vision of your mind you now see
She's there to watch silently
Each mortal eye before her stands
Is she real or just a dream

Men come and go yet there she stands
Who is real she or man
What inspired your mind
That would last throughout eternity

# Change

Contemplate the power of a seed
Planted within some fertile soil
Watered by God's gentle rain
Let the change begin

Who can understand the change
Of its complexity dormant life
Newly activated growing state
Now a living growing entity

Who placed its spirit within
Like the Creator of us all
Who dwells far from within our view
This spirit that dwells within this tree

Lies beyond our human view
Just as real as our spirit within
Each day it seems to stand so still
When we view her growth year by year

We realize her change is not just a sprout
How do you explain the change
When it becomes a mighty grown tree
Timber of every kind for the use of man

Then cut and laid upon the ground
Explain to me the change of this mighty tree
Where O where has its spirit gone
Like man when laid within the ground

It's evident that his spirit has gone
To dwell within another sphere
So, it is with each and everyday
Life is a constant living change

Spirits come and go from sphere to sphere
Yet God remains within his sphere
Organizing one and all to comply
With God's eternal laws

# Does It Really Matter

Does it really matter that God created the world
Does it really matter what you think

Without God's organized matter what would you be
Matter is really at the core of all things

Like the center of the earth with all its matter
Without the sun could we even be organized matter

Did it really matter if Adam ate the forbidden fruit
Was Eve really at the core of the matter

Have you really thought what does really matter
Everything you see is matter

Everything you do not see is matter
If you think that something doesn't matter

Could your thoughts be the subject of the matter
If God created all things did he not create matter

Matter comes in every conceivable form
When Jesus Christ changed water to wine

Was it not the transfer of water matter to wine matter
When Christ said your faith has made you whole

What kind of matter was contained within those words
Jesus Christ is really at the center of everything that matters

Without Him there would be no organized matter
His words are the reason that things happen

Therefore from the words of Christ comes matter
From the mind or from the earth it makes no difference

Matter is the subject to contemplate
Thoughts of the mind bring forth organized matter

Organized matter leads to the Savior of the world
The Savior said, "Come unto me and find real joy"

You explain to me how real joy matters
There is an eternal law that matters

Life is eternal and that is what really matters

# Early Departure

Long before you were a child
You agreed
Your stay would be short
Trials of every kind good and bad
Your mortal body obtained
No need to be tested
Now it's time to come home
Your righteous soul obtained

Your parents secured-- for all eternity
Your imprint-- planted on their hearts
Your message conveyed
Eternally thankful for mother and father
Part of an eternal family
Many waiting on the other side
To welcome you home
So many sad to see you go

Yet many glad to see you back
To reside within your Heavenly home
It was meant to be this journey
That all could be -- an eternal family
Your time would be an
Early departure

# Remember Me When I Am Gone

When I am gone will you remember me
When I am gone
Gather together one and all
May you sing a happy song

Know that I am alive and well
When I am gone
If you cared for me at all
Then tell them of my song

I rejoice in the home of my Father
The spring of all living water
When I am gone
All is well in the land of the living

I have found the source of all living water
Now that I am here my spring runneth over
My joy is full
What more could our Savior give

When in the midst of His presence
No more do I thirst no more do I roam
When in the presence of my Savior
I feel right at home

# Poor of the Poorest

Wealth and fame, have I none
Gold and silver are but a dream
Cool water how I thirst
Land I have none

Shelter but a tent
Abused and abandoned
Family long gone
Old and alone

Clothes worn and torn
Surrounded by wealth
Noise everywhere
Winter is coming, nobody cares

Could life be any worse
The police say I have to go
Cold and wet sick and dying
No place to go

Saw my body under a bridge
How to explain my condition
Who's calling my name

How easy to move and feeling so warm
Could this be my new home

All clothed in white
God has just welcomed me home
Now I remember
I was chosen to be one of His Sons

Poor of the Poorest on earth
Wealth untold
In my new home
Test completed

# Procrastination

The rain soon cometh so they say
Yet they say let it wait until another day
The rain is coming make no delay
They know that's what they say

Are they sure the rain is on its way
Did they see the clouds within the sky
Does that mean it's going to rain
Did they see the lightning and hear the thunder

It made quite a show they say there is no rain
The time is getting shorter each and everyday
They have too many things to do
So they must be on their way

Now that it's raining what are they to do
Water everywhere it keeps on rising
Where is that Prophet and his boat
What did He say about procrastination

Did they hear that Christ is coming
So they say but they think it will be delayed
When Christ comes again within the clouds
What will be their response

Did others not prophesy that He was coming
Did they not see the warning signs
How many days have they left before His coming
What was said about the righteous and the wicked

Does it really matter what they say or do
Time is running out for them to know
Like the prophets old and new it's the same
Repent and be clean

Man's procrastination is nothing new
The rain just keeps on coming
Christ will be here
Sooner than they think

# The Day I Wasn't There

I wasn't there when Adam and Eve entered into the garden of Eden
I wasn't there when Noah built an ark
I wasn't there when Moses led the Israelites out of Egypt
I wasn't there when Rome ruled the world

I wasn't there when Lehi lead his family out of Jerusalem
I wasn't there when Spain ruled the seas
I wasn't there when the Greeks worshiped many Gods
I wasn't there when Jesus of Nazareth was born

I wasn't there when Jesus entered into the garden of Gethsemane
I wasn't there when Jesus hung on the cross
I wasn't there when Jesus was laid in the tomb
I wasn't there three days later when the tomb was empty

I wasn't there when the resurrected Jesus appeared unto his disciples
I wasn't there when Paul was visited by Christ on
        his way to Damascus
I wasn't there when Christ appeared to the Nephites
I wasn't there when George Washington defeated the British

I wasn't there when Joseph Smith went to pray
I wasn't there when Joseph Smith saw the Father and His Son
I wasn't there when Joseph was martyred
I wasn't there when the Holy Ghost came to Christ when
        He was baptized

I wasn't there when the Holy Ghost came upon Christ's apostles

I wasn't there when God sent His only begotten Son to die for us

I was there when the Holy Ghost testified unto me of the
truthfulness of all these things

I was there when Christ filled my heart with joy beyond measure

I am here to testify of the truthfulness of all these things

# The Eagle Has Landed

There was a young bird who wanted to fly
He came from a very good nest
His mother and father O how they could fly
Was not long when he noticed O how he wanted to fly

Why should he try was warm here in his nest
Then came brothers and sisters O what a mess
It was getting crowded within his comfortable nest
Then it was said you should really learn how to fly

He stretched out his wings if only I could fly
Then back he would go with O how I wish I could fly
Then it was heard follow me to learn how to fly
Little by little he tried each time he tried

I think I can fly then back to the nest
Only to say O how I wish I could fly
Others came along each took his turn
You really can fly his mother soon took to her broom

There began to be less and less room
You must learn how to fly so it was he would try
Until one day-- he wanted to quit then this little new chick
Was heard to say you better not quit

There flew into this warm little nest an old mother bird
Thus it was said when she had left I know I can fly
It's not that hard if only I would try
Then flew into his nest this eagle he knew

Come on you're almost there so it was he climbed to the edge
As he stretched out his wings high above within the clouds
Low and behold this old mother bird stepped up and kicked
This young bird right out of his nest he opened his wings

Off into the sky he would go
And of the rest as they looked from their nest
I knew he could fly there came such a cheer
As he soared through the sky O what a sight

As he soared to their nest then it was heard from afar
Of an old mother bird who knew he could fly
Then came these old birds who gathered together
Each sought one another now they waited to see

This young eagle as he soared for their tree
Then he came flying strong as the wind he soared by these old birds
They looked and they waited to see this young bird
As he flew into view then slowly he glided until he had landed

Then it was heard from one and all
This fine young Eagle has landed

# Who's Responsible

Man and his agency mind over matter
Good and evil life and death
Does man really have a choice
Life is a journey with consequences

Is man really free to choose
Who then is responsible
There is no beginning and there is no end
Man's journey to earth was a gift

Life with so many choices
Who then is to say why did they do it
If they came from someplace
Their journey isn't through

If life was a gift from the Creator
Life will last throughout eternity
So where have they gone
Does it really matter why they left so soon

Man and his choices who is responsible
Did they leave their troubles behind
Or did the spirit inherit them all
Agency is a dangerous thing

Man is surely free to choose
So where do they roam
God knows and loves
Each and every troubled soul

Their spirits and their choice still free to choose
Life is a journey to the judgment seat
Who then is responsible for man's troubled soul
Each and every one God will review

Then how can we say they are all wrong
So where do they roam not far from our home
As long as we are not responsible
For someone's troubled soul

We can rest in peace
And leave the rest
Up to God and his wisdom
To help each and every troubled soul

# God &
# Jesus Christ

# Mercy or Justice

They say there is no God
Yet judge ye for yourself
If ye live or die what is your destination
If you live with no God you have
No destination
Your life here is all that you have
You become the product of your environment
No mercy and no justice
Only a very little time to exist
All you can expect is to become a speck of sand
The Creator of Mercy and Justice
Has a very different set of plans
One with an eternal destination
For the journey of all mankind
A world where Mercy and Justice exist
Justice for all of his creations even man
Justice is ruled by laws
Without laws there is no justice
Without Jesus Christ there is no Mercy
Without knowledge of the Creators laws
Men are left to the law of Justice
Without Jesus Christ you have no hope
Mercy is a far better road then justice
Man must choose his destination

# A Vision of Eternity

What can man really see and hear
Why stand and touch a tree
What is real
That you cannot see or hear

Can you hear a mother's cry
In a land you cannot see
Is her anguish any less if you can't hear or see
Can you see God's stratosphere

Your mortal eyes view His stars
They look right through this veil
Yet when debris it comes
You're free to view His heavens

Did you hear or see His Son
When He walked into Gethsemane
Did you hear Him plead for you
Did you see Him bleed

Did you see Him hung upon the cross
Did you hear Him cry to Me
What then is real
That you cannot hear or see

Can you see my air I created for you to breathe
Take a breath and pray to Me
That you might see and hear of things
That exists within My eternity

Can you see your desire and willingness
You have them both
Can you see this thing called pride
Can you hear it say to you no it just can't be

What can man really see and hear
When he only has mortal ears and eyes to hear and see
Let your spirit communicate with Me
Cast off your pride find humility

Will be upon a humble knee
A sincere cry to Me
Then My child I will open up your eyes
That you can see into My eternity

# God's Essential Animals

Milk butter cheese and cream
You learn to milk and churn
Without the cow no butter cheese or cream
Without the milk why learn to churn

Eggs over easy or fried one or two
No rooster no chicks to brood
Hens one or two if not no more stew
Sheep black and white a lamb or two

All for wool for man to card
Mutton for the sheepherders stew
Without these three no need
To milk the cow or feed the sheep

Let alone gather eggs when the hen is all alone
When you set the table give thanks
To God for these essential three
Then set down enjoy your meal

Then go milk the cow
Gather up the eggs
Find the sheep out in the pasture
Bring them in and sheer some wool

Now that you're half way done
Go out and have some fun
Then back to work
For there's lots to do

Plow the field then fix some fence
Water the garden
Hoe some weeds
Now that you're almost done

Gather up a hen or two
For this evening's chicken stew
Milk the cow
For a glass of milk or two

Don't forget the sweater your wearing
Was wool you carded yesterday
Without these essential three
Things would be much different

At each and every meal
Now then let God know
How much you appreciate
These essential three

# God and My Garden

The garden that no one sees
It's Our roses that everyone wants to see
Yet for me it's everything that no one sees
Did you see the hole I made for this rose?

Did you feel the soil I created so the rose could be
Were you there when I thought to plant this rose
Were you there when I pruned and shaped our roses
Were you there when I came in sore and tired

Were you there when God said,
"Let this rose come forth"
What power could bring her beauty
Yet remain such a mystery

Remember my God and I
When you walk within Our garden
It was my God and I
That caused the beauty of these roses for all to see

# God's Heart

When man was created God said
Let's make man in Our image

Since man now has a heart
What kind of heart does God have

Could it be filled with
Humility love compassion

Best of all a broken and contrite one
Most of all a resurrected one

One filled with mercy justice
And a love of all mankind

Without the heart man would cease to be
Without God whose heart would it be

# He Is Coming

He said that he would come again
He left a string of clues and prophecies
They say that time is running out
He said if you love me keep My commandments

How can you keep what you do not know?
How can you know when He is coming?
Why is it important
Who is this Being that we should know

The date when He shall appear
Where shall you stand when He does appear
Who will swing the sword of justice before He comes?
Will your heart fear or rejoice when He comes?

Time is running out so they say
It could be any day for the righteous do not fear
Time is running out for those who do not know
For this Man who said ---that He would come again

The earth will rejoice when He comes
As for man it all depends on where he stands
Could it be that it's too late?
For it takes time to create a righteous soul

Time is running out so they say
For God makes no delays

# Humility

O how the world is in need of it
What is man without it
Who then is the possessor of humility
Humility requires an investigated mind

How does one become a teachable submissive soul?
Could man acquire humility without desire
They first must become a willing soul
Light and truth precedes humility

Humility is a very precious commodity
When acquired it softens a hardened heart
Kindness begins to grow each and every day
Man sees things in a whole different way

Like the Master Teacher who showed us all
Who went into Gethsemane for one and all
Then hung on the cross for all to see
Then buried and rose all because He showed us

How to have humility
Life becomes very precious
Without the Master and His light and truth
Humility remains a hidden treasure
Lost to all humankind

It takes a submissive teachable soul
To have humility for all humankind

# The Boot That Talked

Whoa is me here I sit not fit to wear
My sole worn out my heel so bare
My strings thin and bare yet my tongue it works just fine

Is there a shoemaker to be found
Who can fix a broken sole give new life to me
I thought this day I was through but off to town I flew

Is there hope for this old boot
All broken and worn down yet I heard him say
He'll be like new

So here I sit waiting to be fixed
It's been too long since I walked a road or two
Or gave comfort to the man that walks within my boots

Then the master of repair took me by the sole
Then proceeded to give new life
When he was through I looked brand new

All polished and repaired
I was ready to be worn
Give comfort and protection to the man within my boots

O how good it feels to walk the fields
Give comfort and protection
To the man within my boots

My master and I have walked some miles to be with you
Could you open up your door and invite us in
There is much we could tell

My master has traveled far just to tell this story
Was of a man who came to earth, was put to death then found new life
It was His journey to be the Master of repair

When all broken and worn down they bring to Him
Their broken soul and ask for this repair
Like before He reassures all is well

Come to the Master of repair
Be patient while He mends your soul
You'll be just fine

Give thanks unto the Master
Who gives new life
To a broken soul

# The Earth and It's Two Sons

Each day we see the rising of our sun
Each day we enjoy the warmth of each one
Each day should we not be thankful
That they both exist
One the Creator the other His creation
Each giving purpose for our existence
Without the sun would you or I exist
Without the Creator's knowledge of eternal laws
To organize this universe and its mighty sun
Where would you and I exist
Without God's Son coming to this earth
What would be the purpose of our existence
Like the sun upon the earth in all of its degrees
From the hottest to the bitter coldest
Man chooses where he will dwell
It is with God's Son who gave man his choice
To be the very best or the very worst
Each Son has his part for the benefit of man
One we see each day to remind us of the other
The other waits patiently to see what we will chose
Should we not bask in the warmth of God's sun
Then chose what is best
That God's Son could warm the enter soul

# Vision of Time

What is it that you can't see
God's time or your time
Whose time is it that you can't see
Can you hold it in your hand
Can you put it in the bank
Will it last as long as you wish
Show me your time
How does one see what's invisible
How much time do you have
Have you used up most of your time
Who gave you your time
Will it last throughout eternity
When did it begin
Will it have a pleasant end
Only time will tell
Just like God
Both are invisible
Yet in the presence of God
Your time will speak loud and clear
Then you will see both
Time and God are very real
Give thanks indeed
To Him who gave you your time
Use it wisely
Because it has no end

# The Gift

Hidden deep within the heart of man
God planted these seeds your gifts
Watered with desire then sprouted
With your willingness and hard work

Talents of every kind for you to choose
Who's the master of your choice
That reaches into the heart's desire
This gift of one's own choice

To cultivate develop and bring to fruition
Each and every gift takes time
For his soul and spirit to communicate
Then the mind begins to orchestrate

Your willingness and hard work
Blossoms of your gift soon come forth
It's not just a seed
But a living growing gift

Day by day and year by year
You become this living growing gift
Now developed and mature
It's there for everyone to see

What is a gift if not a growing living entity
That brings pleasure and joy to everyone
Within its far-reaching sphere
When aged and matured beyond one's years

Now you're the giver of your gift
To plant within some souls
Then depart this mortal life into another sphere
Giving thanks unto the Planter of your seeds

Now God and you can enjoy
Your choice of gifts into eternity

# A Speck of Sand

One of God's great gifts a speck of sand
I hold within my hand a glass

Made from a speck of sand
I sat upon a beach His sand to enjoy

Without God's sand we would have no beach
The earth would be so bleak without God's sand

Water and sand they go together
Would it be a beach without the water

Or just some desert's sand
God has placed each according to His plan

It takes time to make His sand
Just like man God had made His sand

Now let man enjoy
Each and every speck of sand

# About the Author

Arnim Nicolson was born in Santa Barbara California in 1938
Received his education in California and New Mexico
Raised in Salinas Valley and encountered numerous occupations
Settled on being a fireman for the next 33 years
Developed a company called Water Tank Specialists
Retired from the San Jose Fire Service in 1999
Married for 58 years, 6 children, 27 grandchildren,
9 great-grandchildren
Encountered several life-threatening experiences
Delivered several babies, one was his own
Served numerous missions within his church
Started writing poems in 2008
Had a strange experience on March 13, 2018
The writing of a poem called Trapped
Had several articles published in local newspaper
Working on his 137th poem and still going strong
Maintains one-acre park at his home in
San Martin, California with his wife

Made in the USA
Columbia, SC
02 July 2023

19891861R00057